ROMANTIC MOV...

for Piano

ISBN 978-1-4234-2568-7

HAL•LEONARD®
CORPORATION

7777 W. BLUEMOUND RD. P.O. BOX 13819 MILWAUKEE, WI 53213

Visit Hal Leonard Online at
www.halleonard.com

BALCONY SCENE

from the Twentieth Century Fox Motion Picture WILLIAM SHAKESPEARE'S ROMEO AND JULIET

Words and Music by NELLEE HOOPER,
MARIUS DEVRIES, CRAIG ARMSTRONG,
TIM ATACK and DES'REE WEEKES

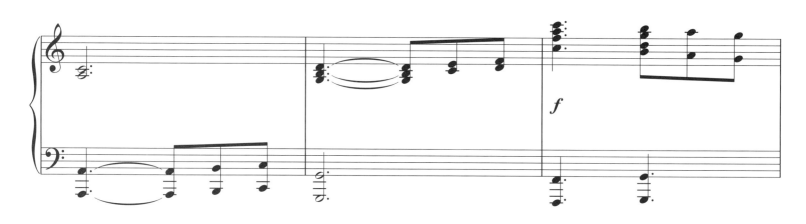

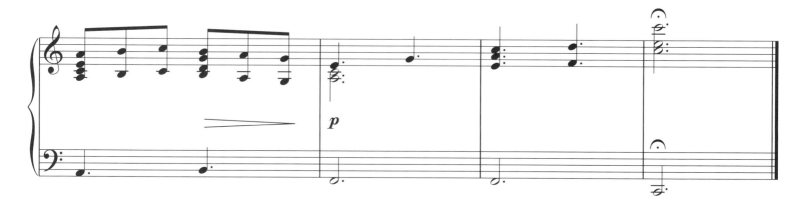

COUSINS
(Love Theme)
from the Paramount Picture COUSINS

Music by ANGELO BADALAMENTI

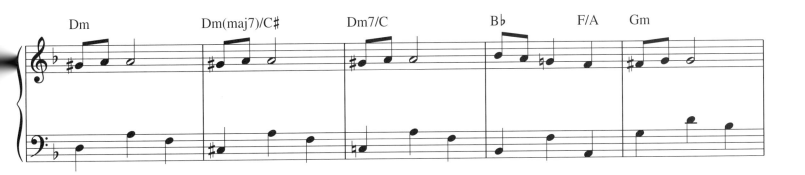

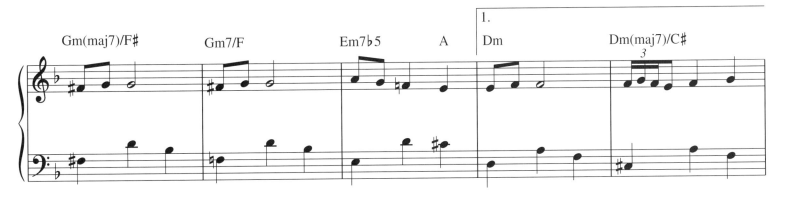

8

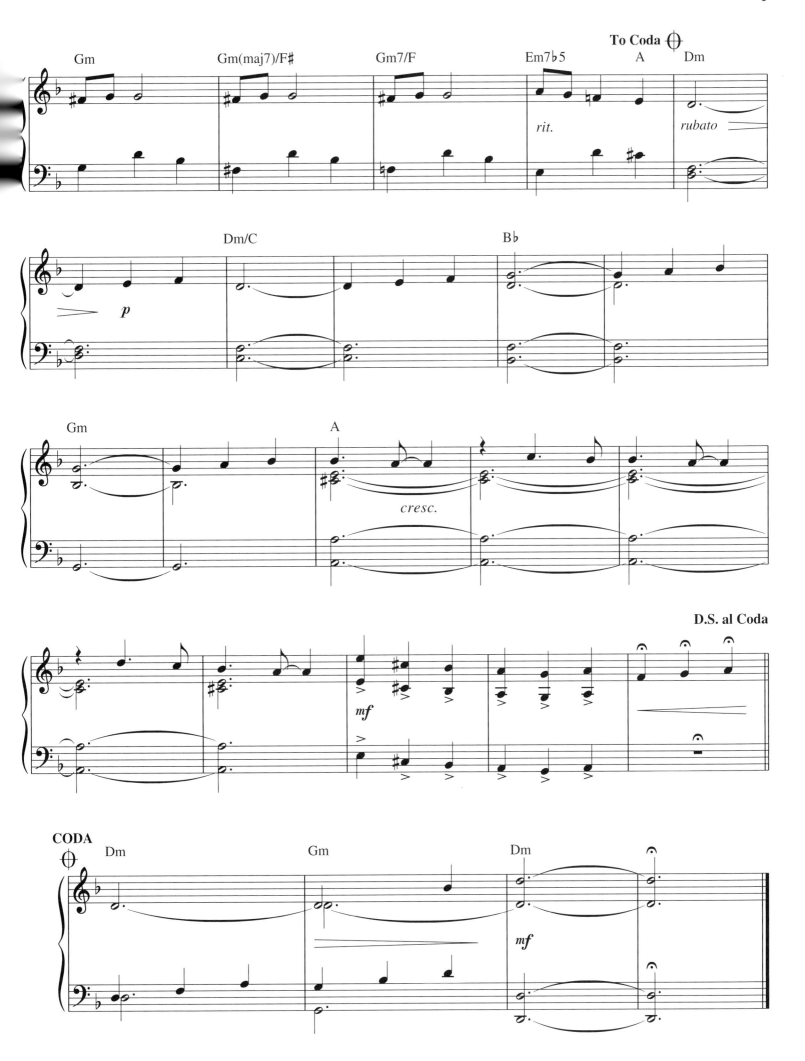

BEAUTY AND THE BEAST

from Walt Disney's BEAUTY AND THE BEAST

Lyrics by HOWARD ASHMAN
Music by ALAN MENKEN

CINEMA PARADISO

from CINEMA PARADISO

Music by ENNIO MORRICONE

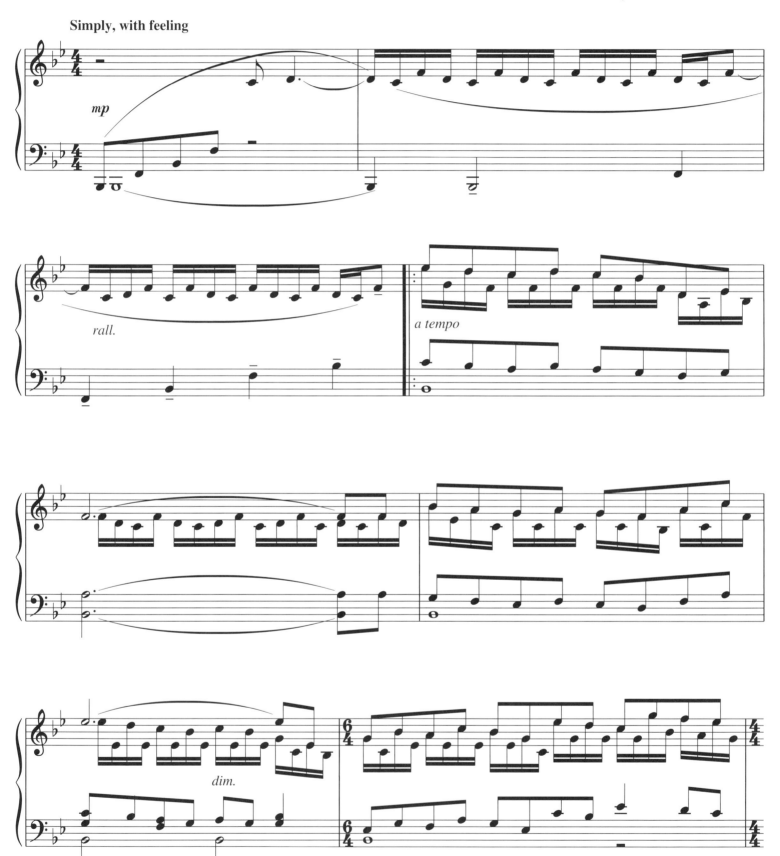

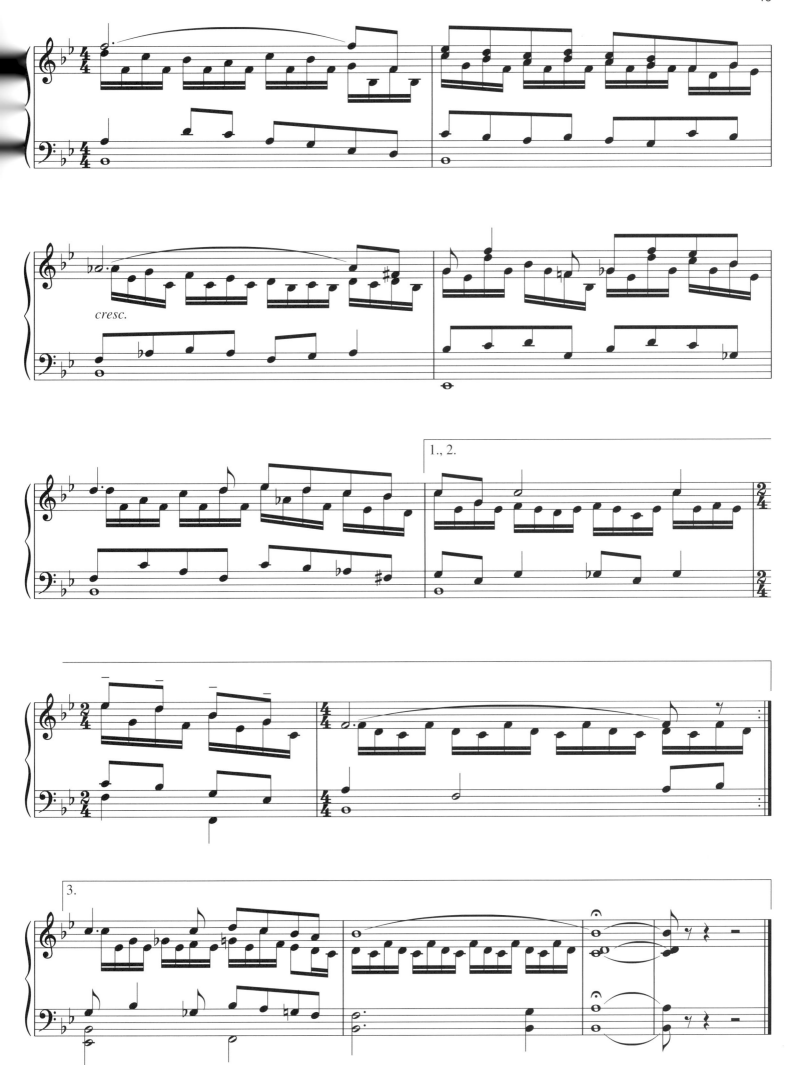

DAWN
from PRIDE AND PREJUDICE

By DARIO MARIANELLI

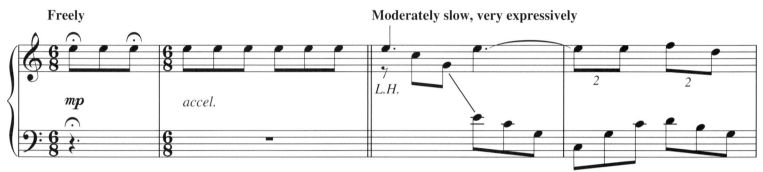

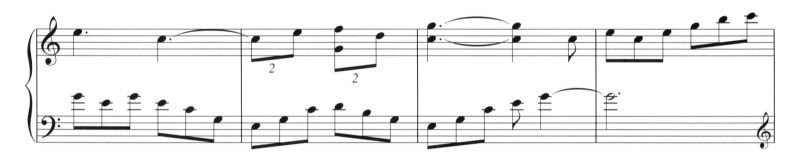

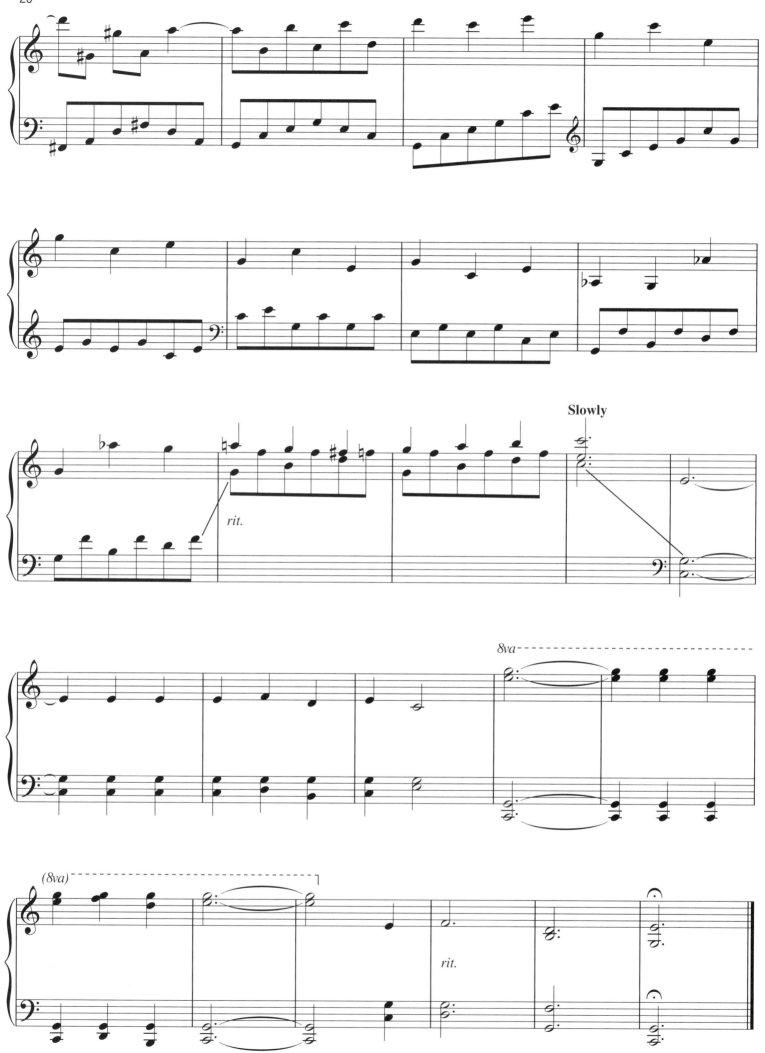

DO YOU KNOW WHERE YOU'RE GOING TO?

Theme from MAHOGANY

Words by GERRY GOFFIN
Music by MIKE MASSER

Slowly, with expression

D.S. al Coda

CODA

THE DREAME
from SENSE AND SENSIBILITY

By PATRICK DOYLE

Moderately, with expression

(Everything I Do)
I DO IT FOR YOU
from the Motion Picture ROBIN HOOD: PRINCE OF THIEVES

Words and Music by BRYAN ADAMS,
ROBERT JOHN LANGE and MICHAEL KAMEN

Slowly, with expression

With pedal

Slower, freely

Look into my eyes, you will see what you mean to me.
Search your heart, search your soul,
And when you find me there you'll search no more.
Don't tell me it's not worth fighting for.
You can't tell me, it's not worth dying for.
You know it's true, ev'rything I do, I do it for you.

Look into your heart, you will find there's nothing there to hide.
Take me as I am, take my life.
I would give it all I would sacrifice.
Don't tell me it's not worth fighting for.
I can't help it, there's nothing I want more.
You know it's true, ev'rything I do, I do it for you.

There's no love like your love, and no other could give more love.
There's no way, unless you're there all the time, all the way, yeah.

Oh you can't tell me it's not worth trying for.
I can't help it, there's nothing I want more.
Yeah, I would fight for you, I'd lie for you,
Walk the mile for you, yeah, I'd die for you.
You know it's true, ev'rything I do, oh, oh, I do it for you.

FOR ALL WE KNOW
from the Motion Picture LOVERS AND OTHER STRANGERS

Words by ROBB WILSON and ARTHUR JAMES
Music by FRED KARLIN

Moderately, with a light touch

FRIENDLY PERSUASION

from the Motion Picture FRIENDLY PERSUASION

Words by PAUL FRANCIS WEBSTER
Music by DIMITRI TIOMKIN

THE GODFATHER
(Love Theme)
from the Paramount Picture THE GODFATHER

By NINO ROTA

Slowly and expressively

LEGENDS OF THE FALL

from TriStar Pictures' LEGENDS OF THE FALL

Composed by JAMES HORNER

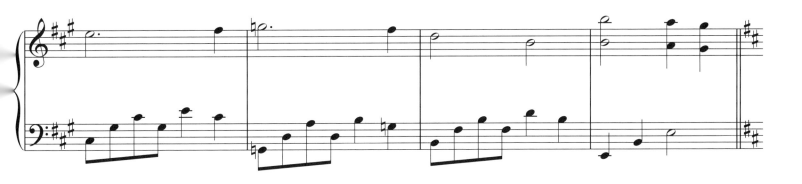

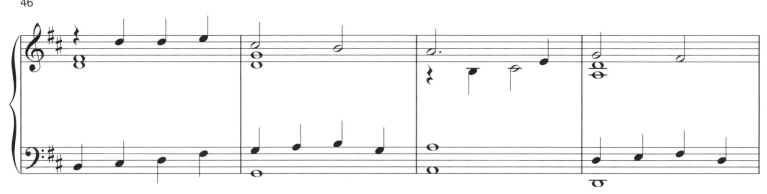

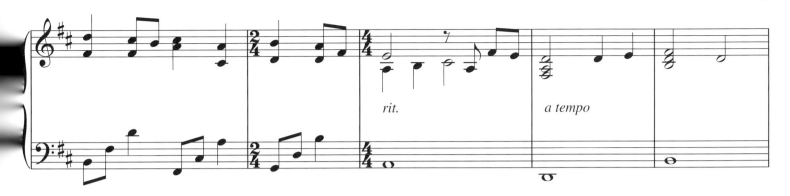

rit.   a tempo

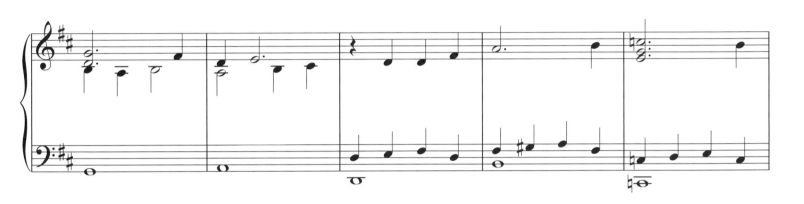

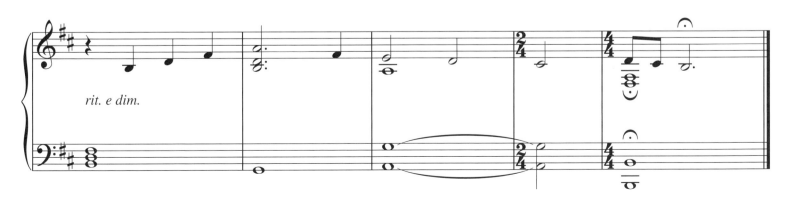

rit. e dim.

HELLO AGAIN
from the Motion Picture THE JAZZ SINGER

Words by NEIL DIAMOND
Music by NEIL DIAMOND and ALAN LINDGREN

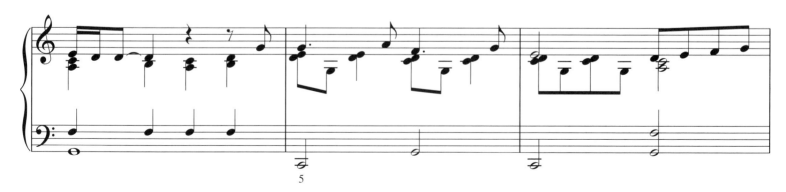

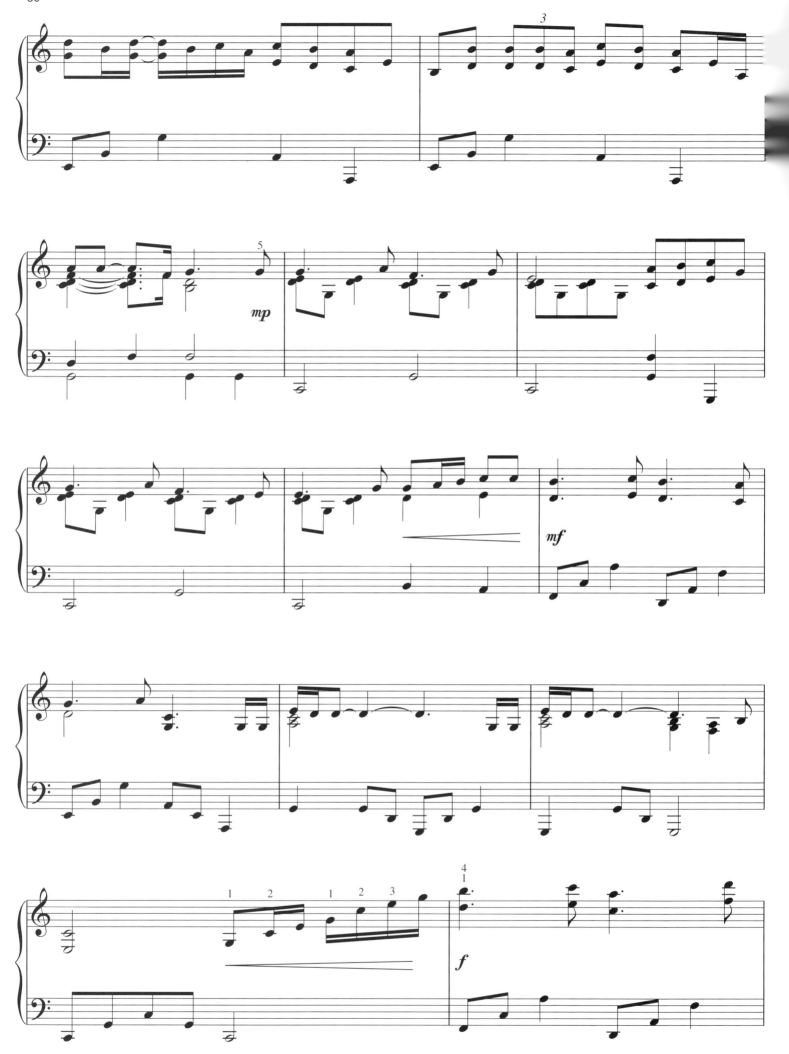

I WILL REMEMBER YOU

Theme from THE BROTHERS McMULLEN

Words and Music by SARAH McLACHLAN,
SEAMUS EGAN and DAVE MERENDA

Moderately slow

IL POSTINO
(The Postman)
from IL POSTINO

Music by LUIS BACALOV

Moderato

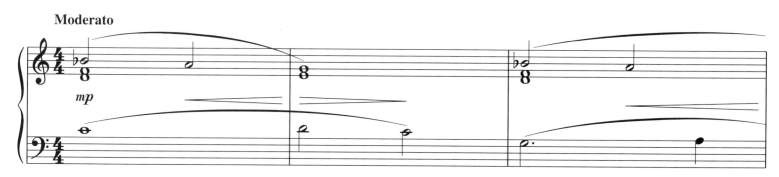

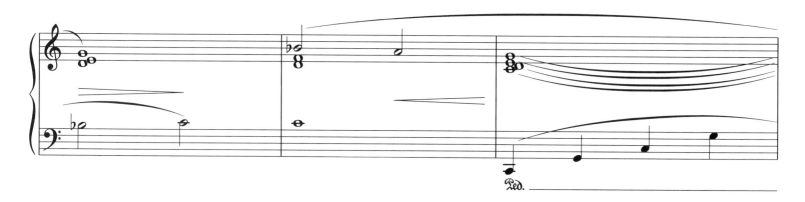

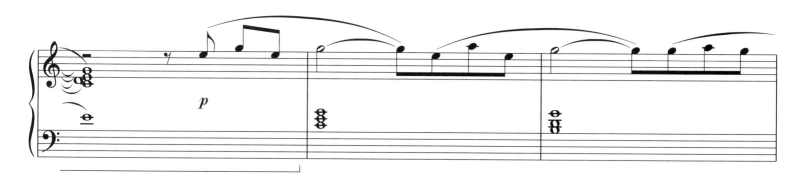

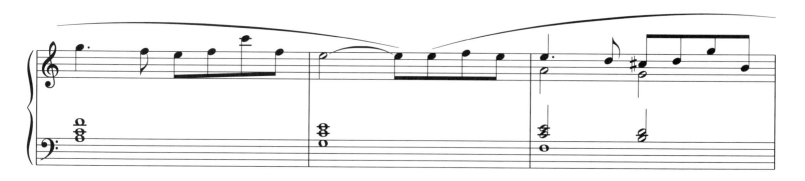

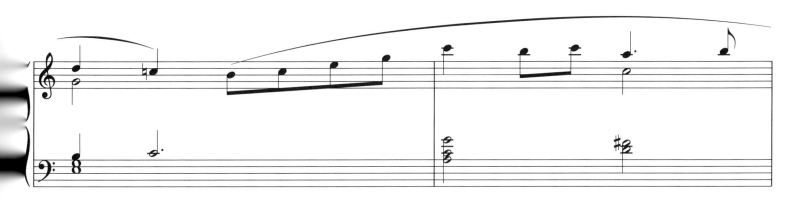

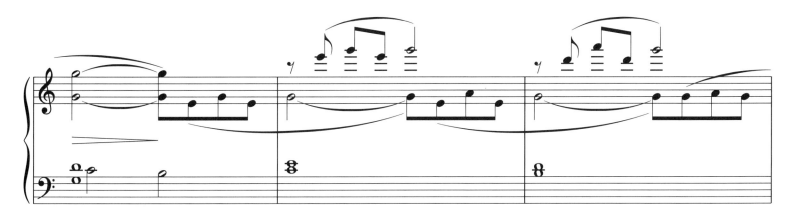

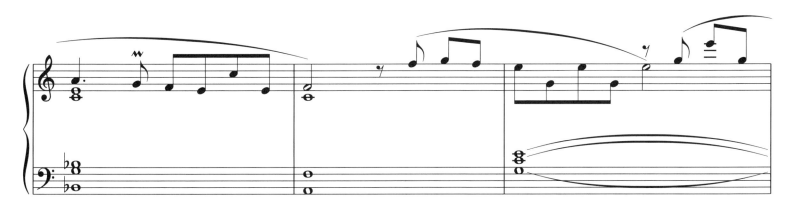

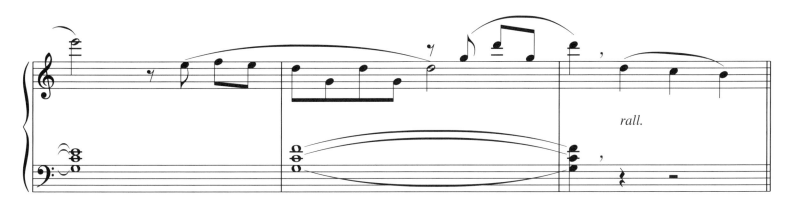

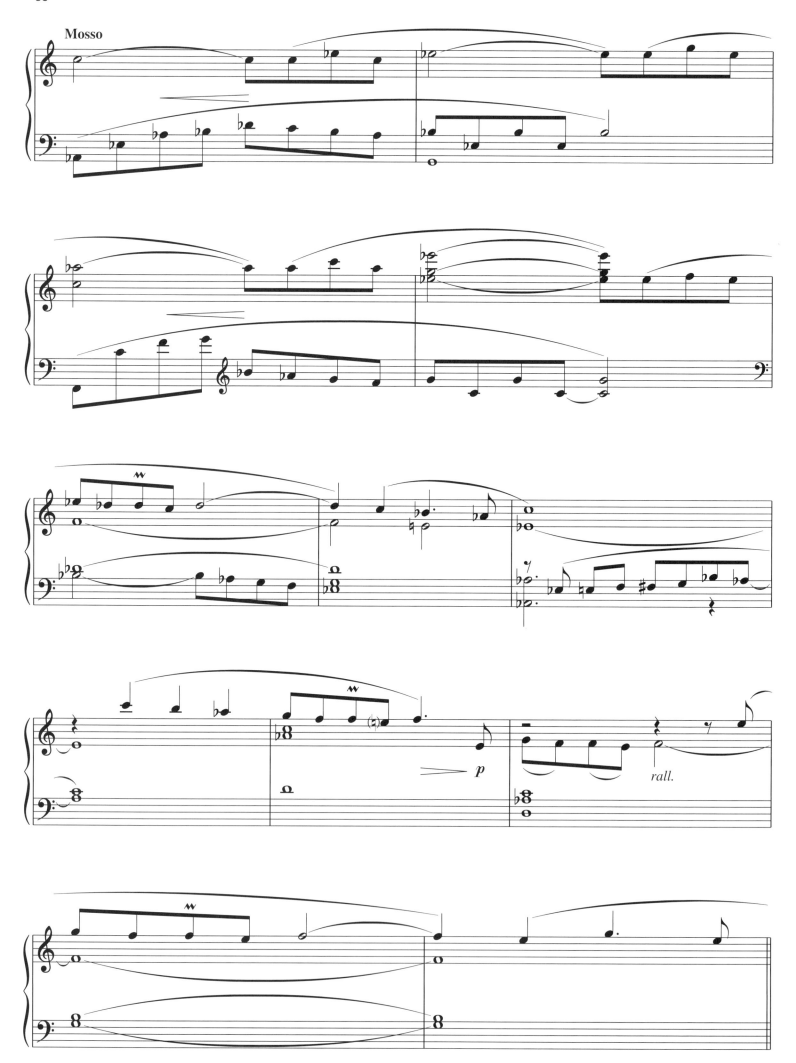

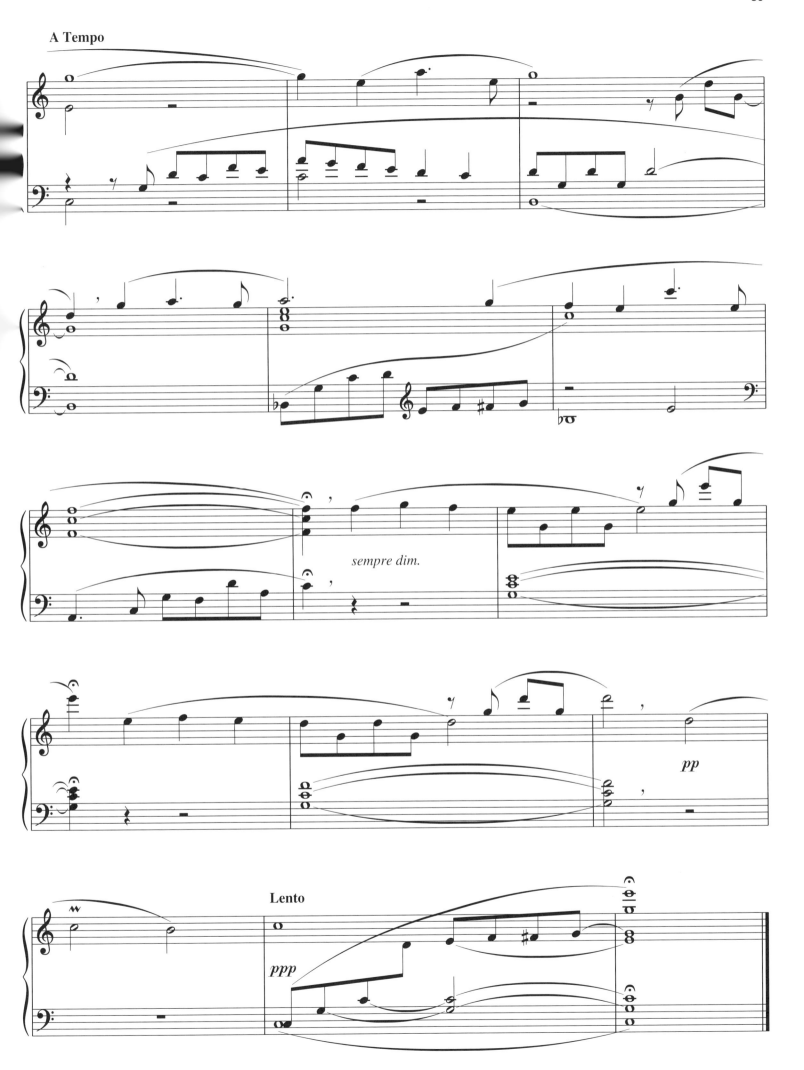

THE JOHN DUNBAR THEME
from DANCES WITH WOLVES

By JOHN BARRY

Moderately

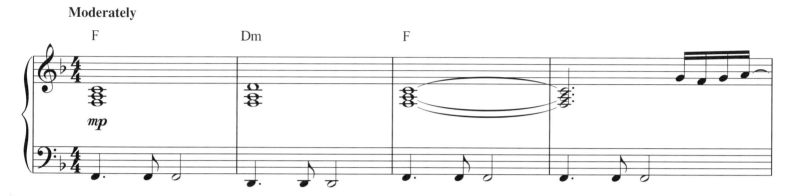

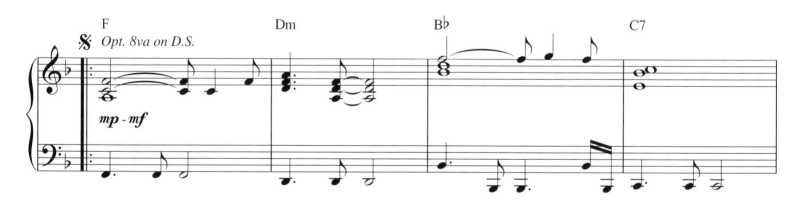

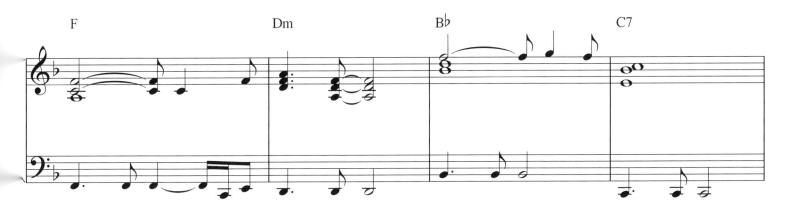

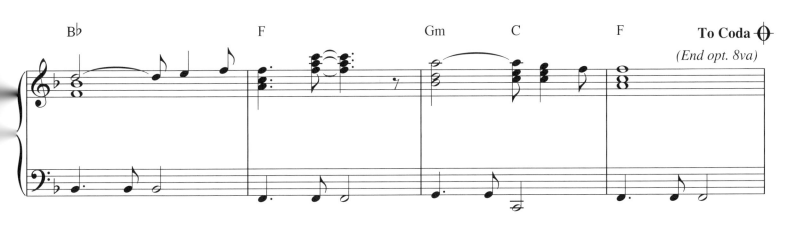

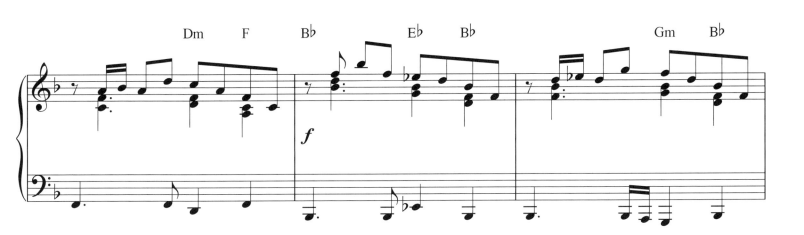

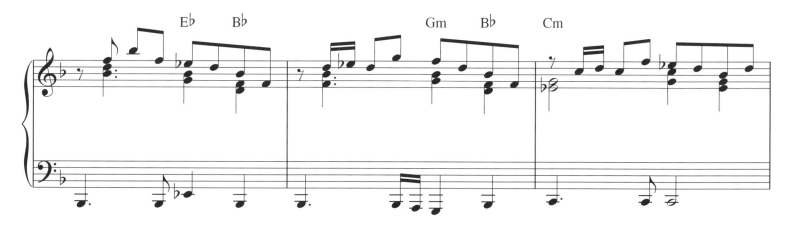

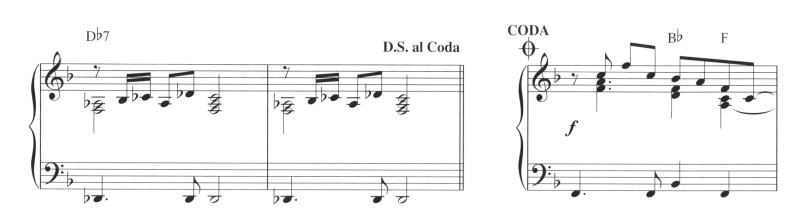

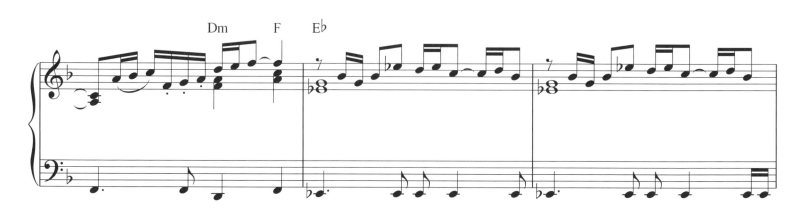

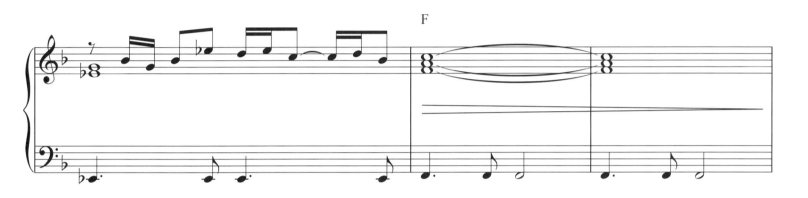

JESSICA'S THEME
(Breaking In the Colt)
from THE MAN FROM SNOWY RIVER

By BRUCE ROWLAND

LOVE STORY
Theme from the Paramount Picture LOVE STORY

Music by FRANCIS LAI

MOON RIVER

from the Paramount Picture BREAKFAST AT TIFFANY'S

Words by JOHNNY MERCER
Music by HENRY MANCINI

MORE
(Ti Guarderò Nel Cuore)
from the film MONDO CANE

Music by NINO OLIVIERO and RIZ ORTOLANI
Italian Lyrics by MARCELLO CIORCIOLINI
English Lyrics by NORMAN NEWELL

Moderate Bossa

More freely

Gracefully

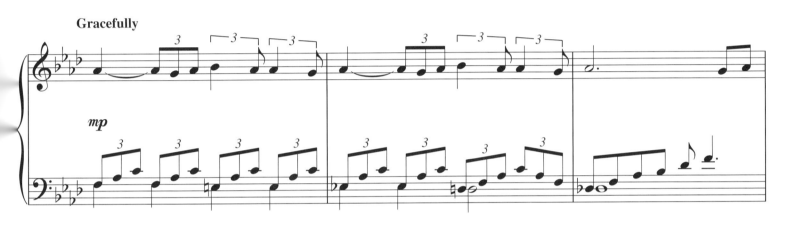

THE MUSIC OF GOODBYE
from OUT OF AFRICA

Music by JOHN BARRY
Words by ALAN and MARILYN BERGMAN

Slowly

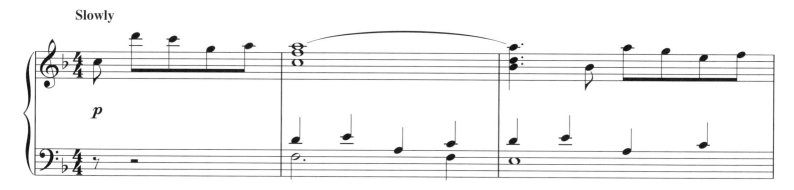

ROMEO AND JULIET
(Love Theme)
from the Paramount Picture ROMEO AND JULIET

By NINO ROTA

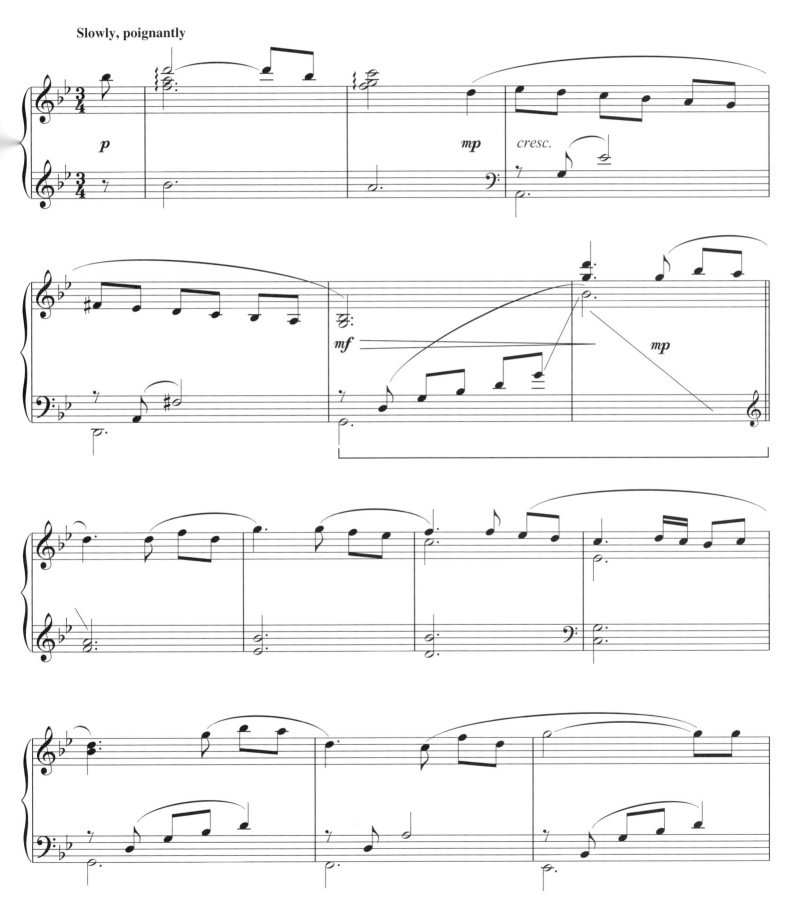

MY HEART WILL GO ON

(Love Theme from 'Titanic')

from the Paramount and Twentieth Century Fox Motion Picture TITANIC

Music by JAMES HORNER
Lyric by WILL JENNINGS

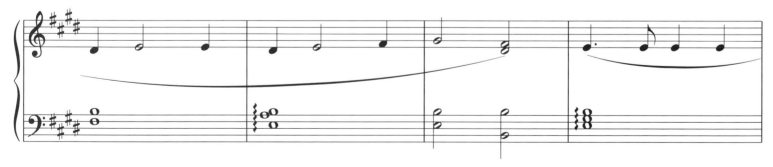

D.S. al Coda

CODA

mp

cresc.

broaden

f

LOVE THEME FROM "ST. ELMO'S FIRE"

from the Motion Picture ST. ELMO'S FIRE

Words and Music by
DAVID FOSTER

SAY YOU, SAY ME

from the Motion Picture WHITE NIGHTS

Words and Music by
LIONEL RICHIE

Slow Ballad

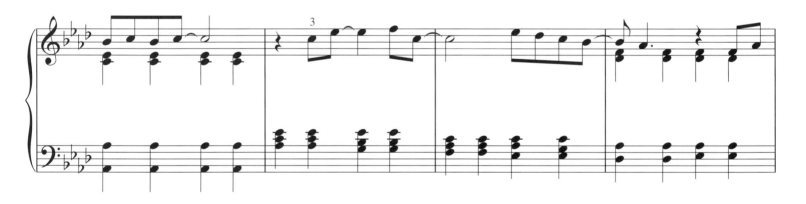

SOMEWHERE OUT THERE
from AN AMERICAN TAIL

Music by BARRY MANN and JAMES HORNER
Lyric by CYNTHIA WEIL

SOMEWHERE IN TIME
from SOMEWHERE IN TIME

By JOHN BARRY

Moderately slow

SOMEWHERE, MY LOVE
Lara's Theme from DOCTOR ZHIVAGO

Lyric by PAUL FRANCIS WEBSTER
Music by MAURICE JARRE

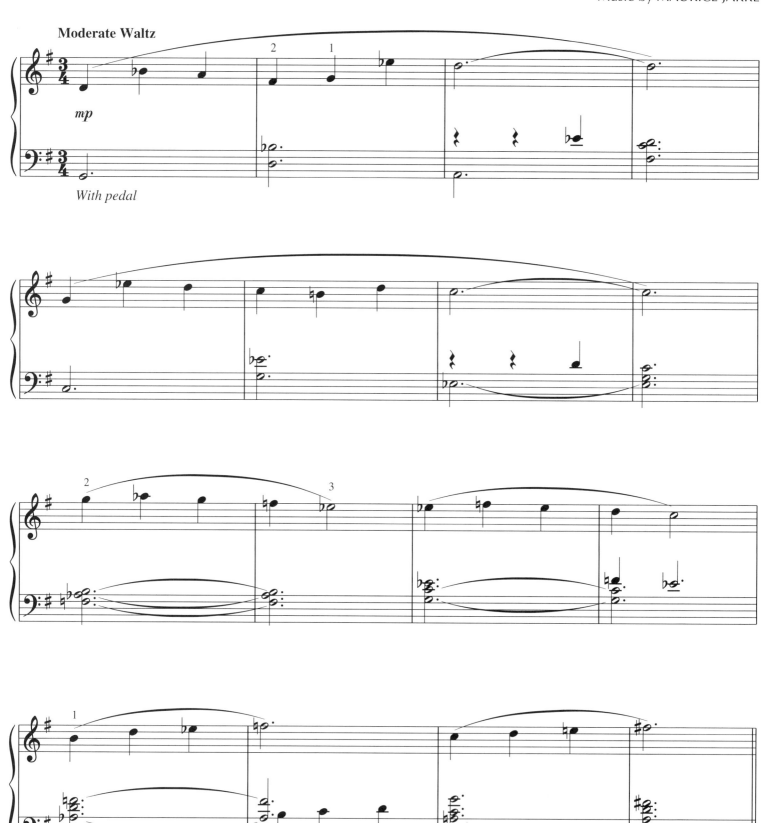

SPARTACUS – LOVE THEME

from the Universal-International Picture Release SPARTACUS

By ALEX NORTH

Moderato

(I've Had)
THE TIME OF MY LIFE
from DIRTY DANCING

Words and Music by FRANKE PREVITE,
JOHN DeNICOLA and DONALD MARKOWITZ

SUNRISE, SUNSET
from the Musical FIDDLER ON THE ROOF

Words by SHELDON HARNICK
Music by JERRY BOCK

Moderately

TENDERLY
from TORCH SONG

Lyric by JACK LAWRENCE
Music by WALTER GROSS

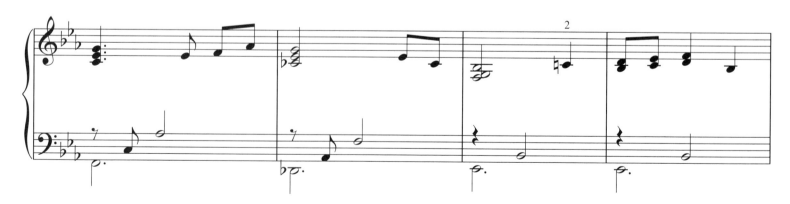

UNCHAINED MELODY

from the Motion Picture UNCHAINED
featured in the Motion Picture GHOST

Lyric by HY ZARET
Music by ALEX NORTH

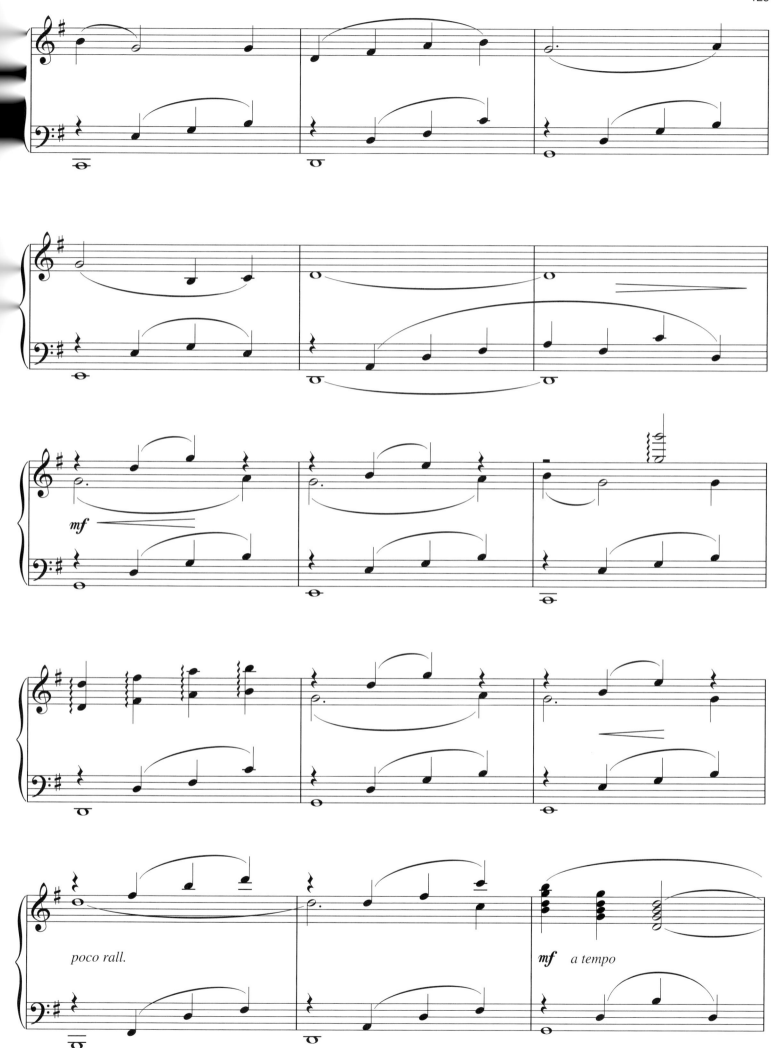

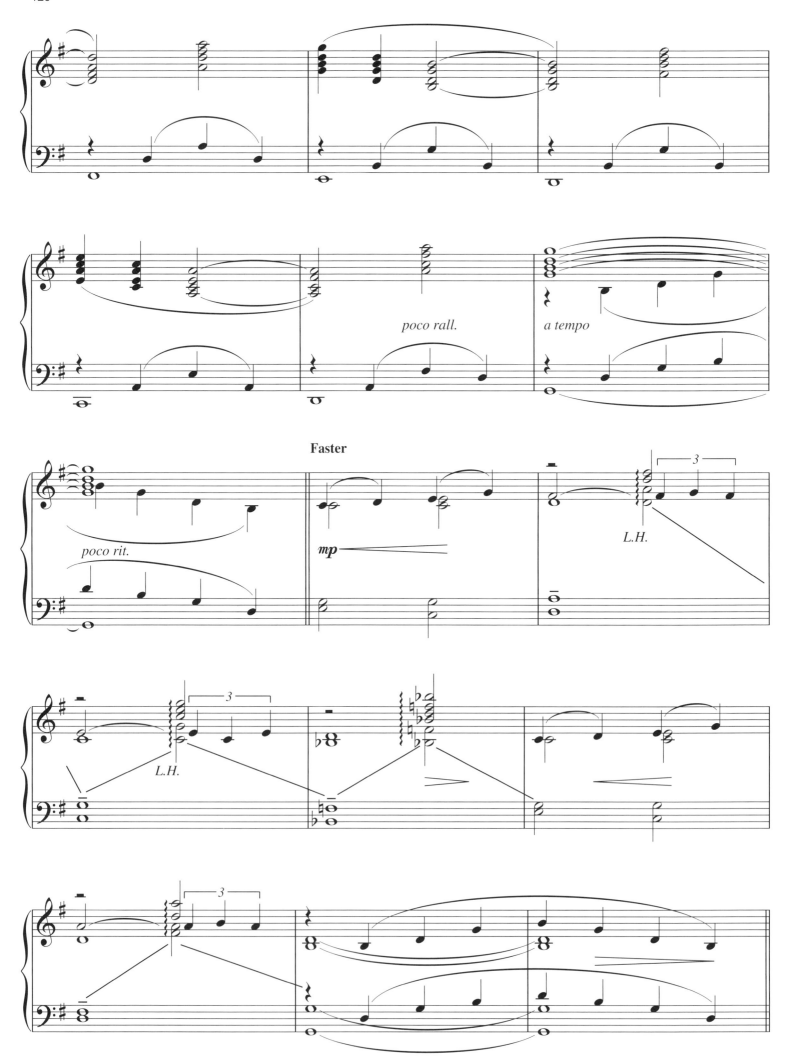

THE WAY YOU LOOK TONIGHT

from SWING TIME
featured in the TriStar Motion Picture MY BEST FRIEND'S WEDDING

Words by DOROTHY FIELDS
Music by JEROME KERN

Freely, in 2

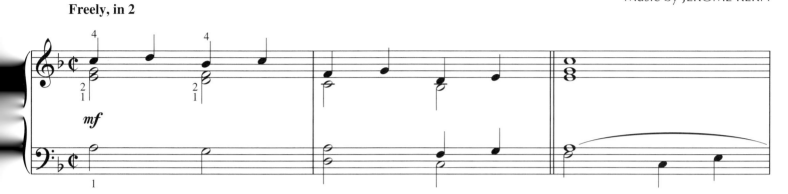

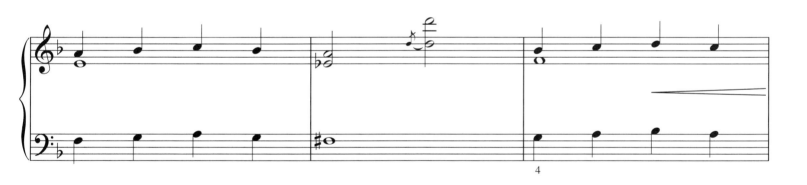

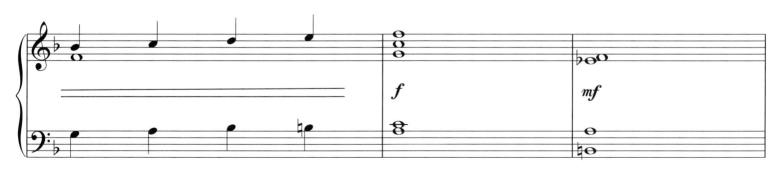

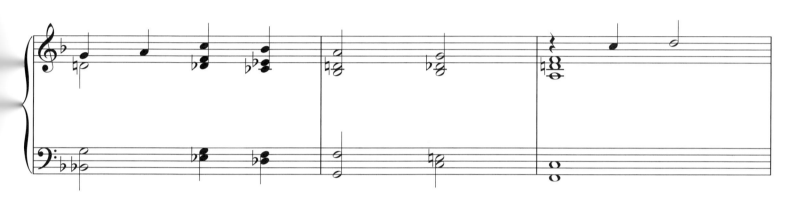

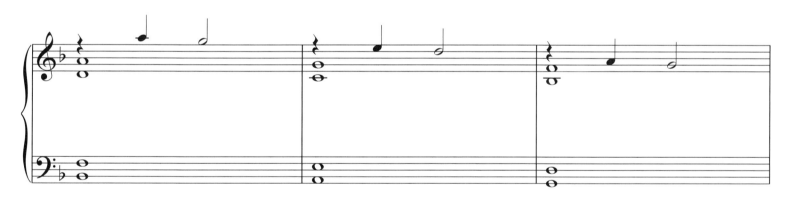

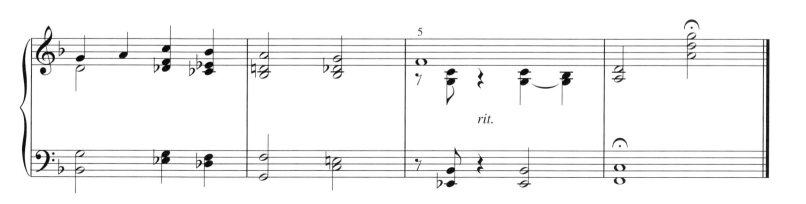

THE WAY WE WERE
from the Motion Picture THE WAY WE WERE

Words by ALAN and MARILYN BERGMAN
Music by MARVIN HAMLISCH

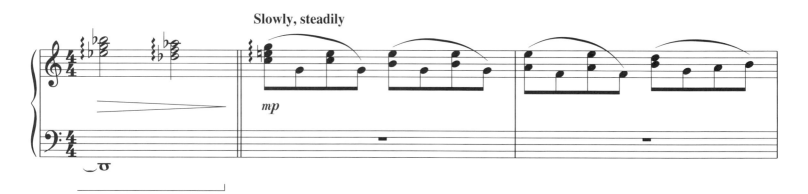

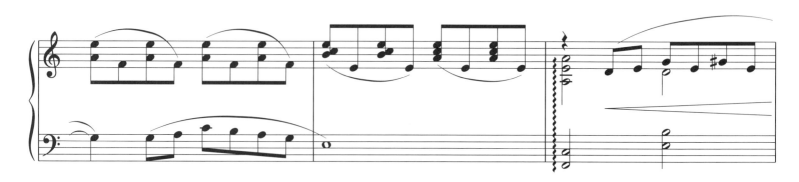

YOU MUST LOVE ME
from the Cinergi Motion Picture EVITA

Words by TIM RICE
Music by ANDREW LLOYD WEBBER

WISH ME A RAINBOW
Theme from the Paramount Picture THIS PROPERTY IS CONDEMNED

Words and Music by JAY LIVINGSTON
and RAY EVANS

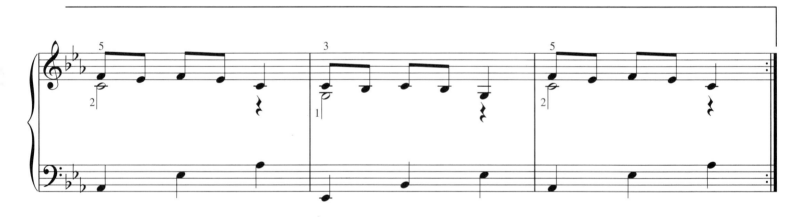